Also by the Autho

If You Like Animals Better Than People

Who's Lucky Here, Anyway?

Who Is Lucky? (bilingual)

All Cab Drivers Look Alike: The Science of Changing Perception Through Experience

Bat Evolution, Demographic Data, and Preexisting Conditions Solve Mystery of Who Dies from Coronavirus Infectious Disease-19

Perceptual Learning and Adaptation

Mystery by the Maple

The Names of Gnomes (& Eileen Abrams, 2025)

**A sneaky stock-market
picture-book for
grown-ups 50+**

DAY
TRADING
for
PREENT

Forest Bae

Illustrated by Felice Bedford and Forest Bae

TIVOLI PRESS
USA . ITALY

Thanks to Javier Alday for technical support.

Published by Tivoli Press, Philadelphia, PA
Manufactured in the United States of America

ISBN: 979-8-9886102-6-7
Library of Congress Control Number: *Forthcoming*

tvp@tivolipress.com or forestbae@proton.me

For my friend Paul 'Coffee-Shop' Bloom —literally;
he wanted to know how I day traded.
And because he has always inspired
the best version of myself.

Preface

How does a poor kid from Brooklyn end up trading stocks? First note, the point is this means anyone can trade stocks, including you. You can stop reading the preface here.

Answer: NYC public school system, Uncle Sam, and the Arizona Daily Star. That's not a punchline, just true. There's also a quilt involved. I visit that quilt in Chapter 5, *Sweet Spot.*

Ditmas Junior High School had an elective called 'Money Matters.' I took it because my brother liked it though he has no memory of the class's existence. The highlight, I was soon to learn, was that each kid contributed two quarters and at the end of the course, whoever's stocks had the most profit got everyone's quarters. We tracked the progress of our picks in every class.

It killed me to hand over that money. Like I said, we were poor. So, as the oversized pages of a newspaper new to me, *The Wall Street Journal,* practically swallowed me up, and with fingers and face smudged in black ink, I studied intensely the stocks and the prices, the companies and their products. I selected a half dozen interesting stocks, reinventing what must have been principles of diversification and undervalued bargain hunting, very determined to win.

I lost.

Can you guess who won? A kid who picked just a single stock – Coca-Cola, a boring, expensive, overpriced, obvious, no-work-involved portfolio. And why did it have to be Richard Cooper of all people? The always cheerful, personable, *affluent* Richard Cooper! He went on by the way to be the class president and I went on to be a scientist; I left the world of uncertainty to others. But I think the experience lit a tiny sleepy spark.

I literally had an Uncle Sam. That was awkward growing up, but I digress. He told me what a mutual fund was, though I was already a professor by then (obviously not in finance!) He learned it from *his* brother. After that, I eagerly awaited every weekly column by Humberto Cruz, financial guru to the Arizona Daily Star; I learned everything I could about the crazy world of money. I even cut out some of the articles and kept them around like talismans. I had a lot of catching up to do.

So, however old or young you are and however much or little you know about day trading it's EASY to start now.

The risks you hear about are, in my opinion, over-exaggerated patronization, the way guardrails are installed at cliffs for the few Darwin-award candidates who don't know not to walk off a cliff. For a senior citizen coyote that is literally, though belatedly, walking off a cliff, see the picture in Chapter 10, *Bears, Bulls – and Elephants.*

The term 'day-trading' can be broadly construed to refer to any buying and selling in the market where you are not seeking a buy-and-hold investment to slowly build your wealth over months and years. Read on to learn how you can buy presents for the grandkids *right now.*

Contents

GRANDPA MOTH

Chapter 1 - Moths

"**D**o you have a moth?"

"What did you say?"

"I said, do you have a moth IRA?"

"That's Roth, not moth!"

"What did you say? Speak up. I can't hear you!"

Sam adjusted his hearing aid with a frown while Paula raised her voice in frustration.

You almost heard right. But this is not a book about IRAs. Or on how saving in a Roth IRA is good for your future. Nor do you have to have one to succeed at what I am about to share in the pages ahead.

I start here, though, in order to scare off anyone under age 50, maybe 59 and a half.

You've earned this. Let them figure it out for themselves.

But if you do have a moth, trading within that account is doubly sneaky and satisfying.

It means no bookkeeping! No having to keep track of purchase price, sales price, number of shares, cost basis, capital gains, Schedule D, Form 8949, capital loss harvesting, specific share IDs, spreadsheets, and accountants.

I bet you thought the answer was no taxes. That too. Not having to pay taxes on any trades means quicker gains and less pressure to push for higher profits.

Anita, Will there be many graphs?

Nah, just this chapter, Paula

Chapter 2 - The Secret

Now that Millennials, Zoomers, and Alphas have all yawned off, I may lose Boomers and Gen Xers too because I am going to start with both a graph and a quiz about it. Please bear with it for just a bit. You can also just focus on the words if graphs aren't in your mental workflow.

Ok, when should you buy this stock? Sell? ... You have learned to buy low, sell high, right? So

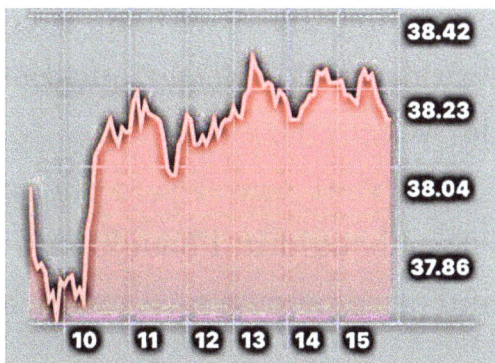

if you had a time machine, you would buy at its cheapest price in the morning and then sell at its highest price in early afternoon. I circled both places in the graph.

But until the day is over, there is no way to know when the stock will be at rock bottom or when it will reach exalted heights - and by then it is too late to trade. It is only in hindsight that you can see what would have been the optimal times to have bought and sold to maximize your profit.

So for those without a crystal ball, what would you do? Better question: What would I do? What DID I do?

On that day, I sold the stock 20 minutes after I bought it. I bought and sold at the times and prices shown next by the blue filled circles.

Apr 2, 2024 at 10:06 AM
37.74
Bought

Apr 2, 2024 at 10:26 AM
37.93
Sold

In the last chapter, Sam needed a hearing aid. In this chapter, you may want to put on your reading glasses. Compared to the peak low and the peak high shown previously, it's harder to see the difference between these two buying and selling points. And that IS the point. You can't buy the low and sell the high without making guesses and taking risks but

you can buy somewhere and sell just a teeny tiny tim higher than somewhere. That's it! That's the secret in the stock market to taking money, not risks.

Tip Toe Through The Tulips

Tiny Tim

Chapter 3 - Surfs up

I like to think of it as riding the waves. When the market goes up, it's clear you can sell higher than where you bought, generating the profit.

But consider when the market is instead flat, making neither gains nor losses for the day. When that happens, it's not like the flatline in a medical drama, here one second and gone the next. Instead,, it hops up and down, up and down.

And even when it's a down day for the Dow, dropping 500 points, it is not the straight descent of a rock thrown off a cliff but more like

Wile E. Coyote going off the cliff - suspended for a while mid-air, then down, then scrambles up a little huffing and puffing before going back down again. (*What? He's in Chapter 10?*)

There are always little up and down waves whether the overall trend is up, flat, or even down. In fact, I love down days and those are specifically the days I like to trade. I will come back to that.

The point is, it works to buy *somewhere* and sell a little bit higher because of those little waves. They guarantee there will always be a little bit higher. The goal is to profit off the local second by second, minute by minute sawtooth movement of the market, not the global year to year or month to month or even day to day trends that feed your 401(k).

Chapter 4 - Every. Single. Time.

Why did I sell at 10:26 AM? And why 20 minutes after buying? Why not a moment later when the price was sharply higher - which would have yielded a much bigger profit - or a moment sooner when it was a little lower? Was I aiming to hold the stock for just 20 minutes? Or is 10:26 AM a good time to sell? Did it just 'feel right'? Did I suddenly get cold feet and irrationally fear the market would go down? Or did I rationally calculate that under these precise conditions, the price was likely to go down?

None of the above. The answer is I always sell when the stock has risen half a percent higher than the price I paid for it. That's it. Every time. Every single time. Every. Single. Time. The mono-word sentences are my imitation of Suze Orman's cadence - though not her message.

I dislike the word discipline, so will not use it here. But I can say that if you do not have the willpower, constitution, or dullness of personality to do this for every single trade, I would  suggest a different hobby. You may want to play pickleball instead of the market.

Chapter 5 - Sweet spot

Why a half a percent? I suspect this amount falls nicely within the zigs and the zags, that quivering of the market I showed you.

You suspect? Don't you know? I don't know because I just wanted a quilt. Perhaps I had better explain.

I was a new professor without any money in the bank and a below-average salary. After five years, I paid off my student loans and grew a bank account for emergencies. Fast forward a little and I had a 'spare' three thousand dollars which I used to make my first ever purchase in the stock market. It was such a

flashbulb memory, I still remember the price I paid for the mutual fund I bought: $16.95 a share. The next day, the price rose and though I did absolutely nothing, I was a hundred dollars richer. I was also hooked.

The power of the market's up and down sputtering waves stayed in the back of my mind. It came to the forefront when I wanted something. The quilt. An overpriced fluffy white chenille bunny rabbit of a blanket. The tufts of cotton reminded me of grandmothers and long-ago lives. But its picture and price tag also reminded me that I did not waste money. If I needed a quilt, which I did not, one costing a third the price was just as warm. And then a thought: What if it wasn't MY money I was wasting?

I purchased Merck stock, my first ever individual stock, with the aim of selling shares after it rose a percent and a half. Commissions for trading were high then and I knew taxes would take another bite, so the expected profit was tiny.

But it worked and after a couple of trades I

had my quilt! Then I 'day traded' – Merck, IBM, AT&T – in order to have the money to hire a financial advisor. He advised me not to day trade and I fired him.

It was more like week trading than day trading though. Frustrating waits with considerable breath holding. It took too many weeks to earn enough to hire the ex-financial advisor.

But what's this? I noticed that not infrequently, the stock price would rise quickly, within minutes, to mere pennies away from my percent and a half goal, only to fall and not return to my target for a week or longer. Should I lower my target?

So I started lowering my target sell price and indeed got faster – but smaller – gains. Much of the time, it started feeling not worth my time. But years later when the commissions charged for a stock trade fell dramatically across the industry, that was a game-changer. Throw in the bookkeeping and tax breaks for trading within a Roth IRA and day trading became irresistible again.

Why not aim for even smaller gains than a half percent? The smaller the gain, the faster and safer the trade. How about a quarter of a percent profit? That would mean selling when the price is only 5 cents higher for a 20 dollar a share stock. An eighth of a percent? That's just a 2.5 cent rise! Ideally, one would sell for a price that was one cent, a mere penny, more than your

purchase price. You will reach your target price faster than you can sip your Chock Full O' Nuts coffee (I'm pretending it's 1932 when their sandwiches really were full of nuts.)

Sure, the profit will be extremely small but then why not just turn around and trade again and repeat again and again and *again*?

To me, this would be true day-trading. I dream of a very fast internet connection – see the eye-opening book *Flash Boys* by Michael Lewis – with a program to automate a multitude of such tiny trades, day in and day out. Even the fantasy crashes into icebergs though, such as not having enough capital to cover waiting for all that trade money to clear; after a sale, your money is tied up for two days to 'settle', though that's down from three a few years prior.

So as a mere mortal, I have found, through trial and error, that a half a percent rise is just right: not so big as to take too long to reach the limit price – which risks a prolonged fall in the market while waiting – yet not so small as to have to be trading continuously. To switch metaphors from sweet spots in racquet sports to one more befitting a stock market with bears lurking: *One half of one percent gain is the goldilocks of day trading.*

Now back to suspecting this strategy works because a half percent is within the toothy zig zags. I never measured it because the idea was stitched together before there were phone apps with easy graphs on demand. The strategy has evolved piecemeal like a patchwork quilt rather than being fully preplanned from the start. Perhaps I will get around to calculating zig-zag sizes before this picture book reaches its happily ever after.

I still have the quilt. I have learned since that it's actually a bedspread. There were a lot of things I did not know back then. The bedspread has been repurposed as a cover for my old couch with holes, which reminds me, I need to day trade for a new sofa.

Chapter 6 - Paint by Number

Stock: Teradata Corp Del.
Symbol: TDC
Shares: 261
Buy: $38.40   *Date*: 4/01   *Time*: 11:41
Sell: $38.59   *Date:* 4/01   *Time*: 1:19
Profit: $49.59

Stock: NCR Alteos LLC
Symbol: NATL
Shares: 502
Buy: $19.93   *Date*: 3/15   *Time*: 10:46
Sell: $20.03   *Date:* 3/15   *Time*: 10:57
Profit: $50.20

Chapter 7 - 9 to 22 minutes

That's how long one trade takes me — between 9 and 22 minutes from the time I sign onto the brokerage website to the time I can sign out. If I execute a second trade in the same session, it adds an additional 5 - 7 minutes. I can't say I'm always thrilled with the return I get for the time I invest. So I aim for two trades in just 15 minutes earning about $50 each. That makes my time worth about $400 an hour, the equivalent of what I earn as an expert witness (on eyewitness testimony) and what my attorney charges...well, used to anyway before he raised his rates.

Money really does go to money. If you have enough assets with your financial institution, you can also trade on the telephone with a real live person, free of any commission.

Otherwise, the phone perk costs a little of your profit. But I have to say, it is a bit of a rush for an erstwhile poor kid from Brooklyn to phone a broker. Though I once dreamed of living in California where I was told hair gets blonde from the sun, (Done! Semester in Berkeley) I never imagined I would one day have a broker I could call and instruct to buy and sell stocks. For extra fun, tell them the process is taking too long to seize fleeting market opportunities.

Electronic trades have been free for a while though. These days, I usually do trade electronically using Wi-Fi on my phone from the comfort of my chenille-covered old sofa.

I am going to go

through in microscopic detail what happens during the 15.5 +/- 7 minutes from start to finish. I don't like when cooking shows start with neat little bowls of pre-chopped pre-measured ingredients as if preparation wasn't difficult. Then half an hour goes by in a minute. *Poof*, as if by magic you have mushroom soup. Real life is messier than smoke and mirrors. A true step-by-step takes nothing for granted and shows something can be done by mere mortals, not magicians. If the details are obvious, skip ahead.

The first part of the time is spent entering the URL for the website, then username and password. It's followed by getting the verification code for two-factor security authentication, which always manages to be on my other phone in another room. I navigate specifically to my Roth IRA and scroll down to one of my fave stocks. I keep a very few shares in the account of my fave day-trading stocks to make the trading faster but you do not have to.

Then it's scrolling to the right – small phone screen means you cannot see everything – and clicking on 'Trade', and further on 'Buy'. A new screen appears and shows the current price per share, such as $37.92. "Echo", I say to my trusty Amazon Echo assistant, "What is 10,000 divided by 37.92?"

"Ten thousand divided by 37.92 is approximately 263.7131." Is it my imagination or is she speaking slower than usual?

"Echo, *repeat!*" I respond, flustered by the many unnecessary digits I hear after the decimal point, her dragged-out speech wiping out memory of what came before. I mentally rehearse, "264, 264, 264," as I select from the drop-down menu that I want a market order and finally enter 264 for the number of shares.

A preview pops up that the estimated cost will be $10,010.88 as well as reminds me of the stock I am about to purchase, its current price, and the number of shares selected. Sometimes at this point I will quickly check the built-in stock app on my phone to look at what the price has been the rest of the day. I allude to

this further in a later chapter. Clicking on 'Submit' seals the deal.

Congratulations, you are now the proud grandparent of a bouncing baby stock! It's a boy!

We're not done. I then scroll all the way down to small print that reads 'View Open Orders'. Another click there to confirm the order has 'executed' along with the price I ended up getting, which may be a little higher or lower than the estimated price, depending on how quickly clicking took for that trade. Whew! Seems like that took too long.

But the real scrambling begins now! As soon as the stock purchase executes, I quickly re-engage my friend, "Echo, what is a half a percent of 37.95? (actual purchase price) "Uh oh, where's my pen? Here it is, "Echo, repeat."

"Sorry, there is nothing to repeat."

Sigh. "Echo! What is a half a percent of 37.95?"

"Half a percent of 37.95 is zero point 1898."

"Echo, what is 37.95 plus 0.1898?"

"37.95 plus 0.1898 is **38.1938**"

So now I have the price at which I want to sell, though I did leave out that I usually do have to say 'repeat' a few more times. Fortunately, you do not have to wait at the screen, fingers hovering at the ready as if you were nabbing concert tix. At least this part of the process is conveniently automated for you.

As quickly as I can, I navigate back to the tab to arrange this trade. I say quickly because the price had already risen another 3¢ in the time elapsed since the purchase. It's probably irrational but I cannot rest until I have locked in the new sell order lest the bouncing baby becomes a bratty toddler before I can unload it.

Navigating back to the transact screen to trade the same stock is needlessly slow. You would think it would be one simple click away but it takes at least four, often requiring substantial scrolling, depending on the method you choose to try to immediately sell the very stock you just bought. The brokerage is

optimized more for the buy-and-hold mind.

Once you are back in, then it's easy on the familiar popup to select 'Sell' this time and enter the same stock symbol and number of shares. I always lose a couple of minutes and gain a couple of gray hairs double checking the number of shares I just bought to make absolutely sure I don't make a mistake.

In addition, instead of instructing the trade be done ASAP, I indicate to sell only when it reaches a certain price. In other words, I just selected 'Limit Order' rather than the any-price immediate 'Market Order' I chose for buying the baby. I enter that price I just calculated, either reading from the paper or the note app I scrawled it on – or by asking Echo to calculate it yet again. I finally select the option specifying the limit order stays until I cancel it (or for 60 days, whichever comes first) before clicking on 'Preview' and finally, as quickly as I can, on 'Submit'.

We now return you to your regularly scheduled program. with apologies for making this sound so much harder than it actually is. I breath out and go back to whatever I was doing before the 15-minute interruption. It's fun. I feel accomplished. Exhilarated even. But...

...It helps to meditate.

Chapter 8 - Goldilocks and the three bears - and bulls?

There are other just-right Goldilocks sweet spots besides aiming for half a percent gain. Some may be different for your needs. Others are strategies to benefit all traders. Still others may be the equivalent of wearing lucky underwear. Remember trading was to get stuff, not tenure. So I undoubtedly accumulated superstition along with strategy. If it ain't broke, don't fix it. So I will tell you every trade-bit I use. I will though spare you cartoons of seniors in underpants – mostly.

It's a bird! It's a plane! It's...I forget.

Trade $10,000 or $5,000 on one transaction. With a half percent rise and zero commission that is a profit per trade of $50 and $25, respectively.

Reason: This guideline started because I was comfortable losing these amounts. That is, I reasoned that if my reasoning had been wrong and riding stock waves was risky gambling, not overlooked loophole, then I could live with the consequences of even catastrophic loss. Plus, $50 and $25 profits accumulated fast enough for my pursuit of trinkets, striking the perfect balance (for me) of potential risk, however unlikely, to reward.

Do not have more than two trades and/or $20,000 open at any one time.

Reason: As above. Also, this limits the amount of cash tied up in day trading. Even when trades settle, you may not want more than a certain amount sitting around in cash reserves doing nothing. The zone of comfort became not more than 20K; these days just

16K in spare cash in the moth IRA. $5,000 did not generate enough profit and $30,000 felt too wasteful.

Initiate the buying and selling plan when the market is down.

Reason: Although the little waves are there to be ridden whether the market is up, down, or in between, I am not an expert surfer. It seems sensible to avoid even a small risk that a big down-turning tidal wave just the second after you buy will drown us little fishes navigating the little waves. If you start when you know it's lower than the crest, you increase the odds of a speedier ascent to the tiny rise you seek.

I am guessing the guru of frugality would agree. As Warren Buffet says: "Whether we're talking about socks or stocks, I like buying quality merchandise when it is marked down."

Corollary: How much lower than the crest before trading feels irresistible? Since I am aiming for a half a percent rise, when the market has fallen at least a half a percent, I take notice. The more it falls, the greater the likelihood I will want to drop everything and take a 15-minute break to trade. 1% is better, 2%, 3%, even more so. My enthusiasm is more likely to turn to action if there have been several days in a row with a market loss. On the other hand, if the market is taking back a half a percent after three days of solid gains, I do not consider that a down day that justifies trading.

Stock apps, often pre-installed, or asking Alexa are two convenient ways to check stock prices as often as desired.

Do not buy if current stock price is too near the 52-week high or 52-week low. These are numbers you can easily see in the same stock app without even having to click.

Reason: Being near the limits may cause quirky stock behavior that preempts the little rising ripple you're waiting for.

You would think if it is near its low for the year then surely you're increasing odds it will rise? But no. You are seeking normal average everyday-Joe stock behavior; your strategy is to fly under the radar, I mean over the sonar. Whatever unsavory news sank it to its lowest low in a year may sink it lower still.

Which brings me to minding the next of our p's and q's - or is that S & P's?

Check the news for the stock you are considering buying.

Reason: To make sure it's falling only because everything is falling.

Maybe it's sinking because the market is down AND there's some bad news for the company. Sneaky. It's easy to miss when there is a double cause. We all assume parsimony: One problem, one cause.

With enough knowledge, presumably news can be used. For instance, perhaps a downturn is especially fleeting when solid earnings for the quarter fell a little short of analyst estimates but lasts longer when the messenger tells us instead it's another year without profits. Or perhaps it's the other way 'round. Beats me, so I don't take chances.

I look for newsless dips – or rather nothing specific to the targeted stock. The market itself flails around in response to all sorts of news – consumer spending, inflation reports, anticipated interest rate changes, another government shutdown threat, election news, chip shortages, European politics, and Martian invasions. Good. The jumpier the market, the more bubbles in its wake.

A quick glance at the latest news for the stock is easy by scrolling down in the app although lately the date has been missing. To be sure, it can be worth *Duck Duck Going* the headline.

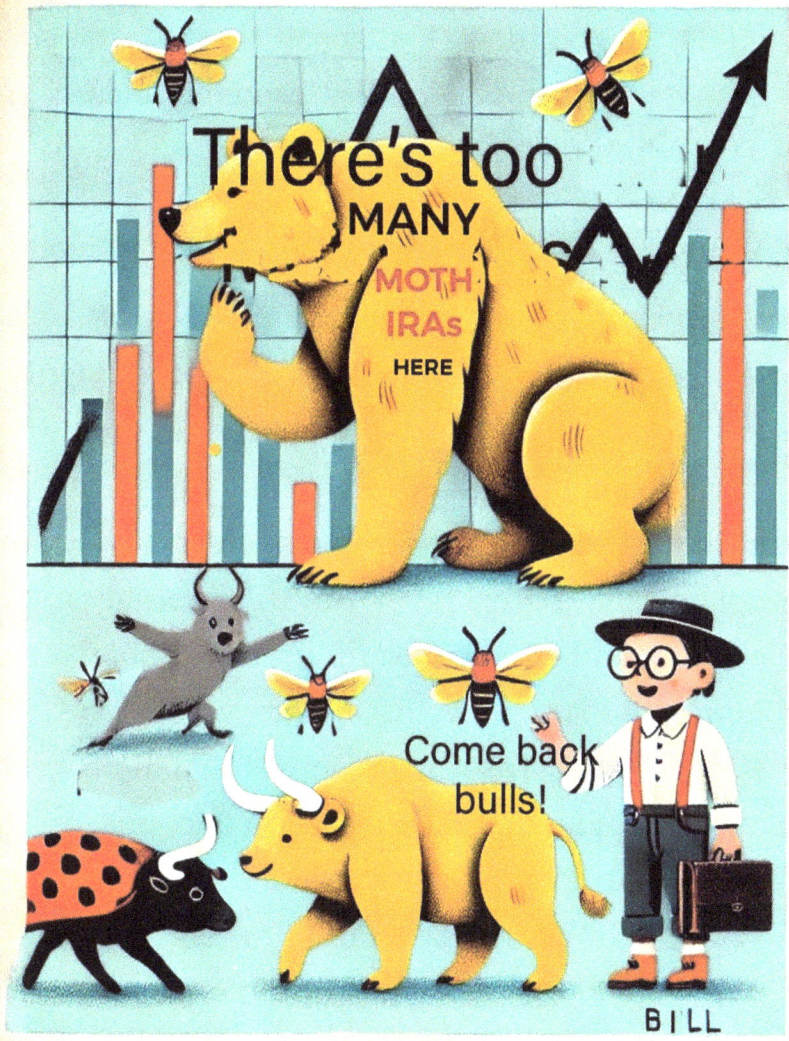

Round down not up. If \$21.4299 is the calculated sell price for a half a percent gain then enter \$21.42, not \$21.43.

Reason: I have had too many just barely made fast trades. I suspect the sweet spot becomes bitter fast and is probably closer to 0.049 than 0.5%.

No-Trade Fridays. I do not buy stocks on Friday.

Reason: Religious observance. Only kidding. During the week, the market seems to have a memory. The price of a stock today is highly related to the price yesterday. I prefer not to hold a stock over the weekend because come Monday, it is as if it is a whole new market. Pick your metaphor; whether it is clean slate, reset button, or Alzheimer's, avoiding Fridays is a good way to minimize getting caught in a reset in the event the stock you bought does not sell in minutes.

Might the Monday market makeover reset in your favor? Sure, but I am not in this to gamble. If I avoid mixing losses with gains, I will reach my goal faster, this year to fund trips to see my favorite wolf. For trades, my favorites are Tuesdays and Wednesdays.

Just like I avoid the ends of the week, I am also cautious about the ends of the day.

Reason: The market is too crowded then.

The first half hour of trading is especially active. What you would like is for a bunch of people to buy your stock and drive up its price while you manage to buy right before that. And to sell at its peak, you want to sell before anyone else. So everyone is trying to do what they think others will do but a split second before they do it. Rushing to be first in line causes a feeding frenzy. Prices are often rapidly and sharply different in the first 15 minutes of trading. Whether I try market or limit orders, I cannot win at this game.

Who wins? I suspect it's those who pay megabucks for the privilege of superfast wired connections to Wall Street. The book I mentioned earlier, Flash Boys by Michael Lewis, is a fascinating look at the extraordinary amounts of money and hijinks that went into building the physical infrastructure to make trading possible a fraction of a second faster than the competition. This included winding wires through people's properties and even carefully selecting the walls where computers would be placed just to get two feet closer.

I prefer calmer sharkless water.

Buy when everyone sells and sell when everyone buys. But everyone is trying to outthink everyone else in a high-stakes game of rock paper scissors. When are you most bright eyed and bushy tailed? When do you think you would be ready and eager to trade? Have the answer in mind? Well then don't trade then. I have been experimenting lately with trading when I LEAST feel like it in hopes some

others who are sleepy won't bother to trade, even if they know they should.

Studies in Industrial Psychology have found midmornings to be the most productive time of the day. Does trading at other times produce a quieter market where there is more space-time between the little waves for the average-speed computer connection to seize? I do not know and for now I mostly just avoid openings and closings while being mindful of times of day and states of mind.

And despite the four time zones in America, I think I spy a time window when everyone is selling. Another project for analysis when I have a long weekend.

♫ Eenie Meanie Minie Moe
Catch a tiger by the toe
If he hollers let him go
My mother said to pick this one
and I choose
Y.O.U.

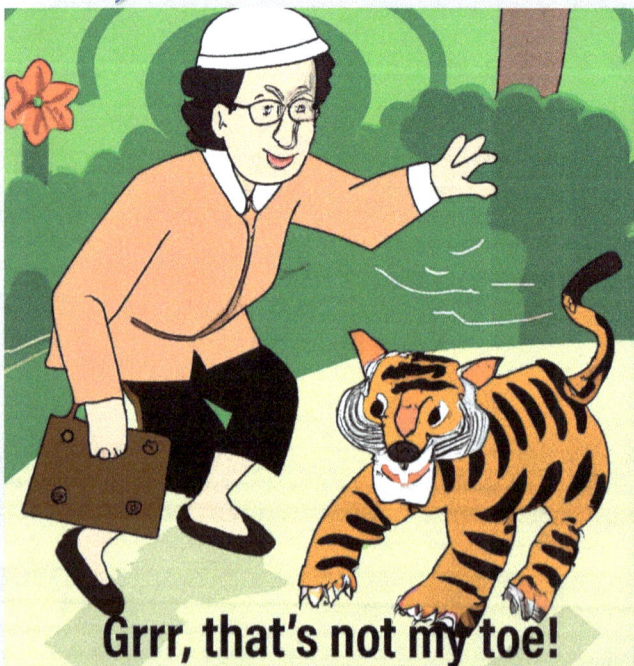

Grrr, that's not my toe!

Chapter 9 - Eenie meanie minie moe, with which stock will you go?

Meds, phones, and computers. Everyone needs those, right? Or so I thought when I first started day trading with buying Merck, AT&T, and IBM. Now I have to look up to remind myself that AT&T stands for American Telephone and Telegraph Company and IBM for the International Business Machines Corporation, originally known as the Computing Tabulating Recording Company. 'Merck and Co', has always been a leader in pharmaceuticals. These three American classics were founded in 1885, 1911, and 1891 respectively, some say 1850 for the big pharma.

My thinking had been: Let's say the trading strategy goes terribly wrong and the Great Depression 2.0 hits the moment I go fishing for a wispy cotton quilt, I mean bedspread. Would it be so terrible then to hold on for dear life to these three great rocks in the financial waters until the economy went back to normal? This was in the days before we knew behemoths like WorldCom could crumble and famous banks nearly so if not for government intervention.

I was also in love with the Merck Manual the way others were in love with rock albums. The book was an increasingly fat text published by Merck every few years since 1899, perfect for one-stop shopping for DIY medicine wannabes ahead of their time. That's why Merck (symbol MRK) became my first-ever individual stock.

The problem with big rocks is they do not move easily. And when they crash, they can stay that way for a long time. Exalted companies fall from grace with the sea following drug recalls and phone snafus. You may have noticed that the stock symbols for the day trades mentioned in chapters 2 and 6 were not T, IBM, or MRK.

I switched away from the 30 (right now 28) largest publicly traded companies that comprise the Dow Jones industrial average, like IBM and Merck, to pick instead day-trading stocks from among the 88 technology companies of the NASDAQ stock exchange. Tech stocks up-and-down price waves over the course of a day seem especially frenetic yet are generally no less safe than those I once thought were pillars of the earth.

Although tech stocks sell for very inflated prices compared to what they currently actually earn, I do not consider them to be unduly risky. They are found in nearly every 401(k) and traded heavily.

Additionally, I narrow down the list of candidates further to companies that cost between about $20 to $40 a share to own. Higher priced stocks tend to take longer to budge a half a percent while lower priced stocks inch too close to risky for my risk-averse make-up. Goldilocks has returned.

For a while now, I have favored TDC (Teradata Corporation, data management for science) and NATL (NCR Altos, banking solutions) when my long[time favorite NCR Corp, which once stood for National Cash Register, split into two pieces. Since I only need two trades open at any one time, I tend to trade these over and over and *over*. Save your creativity for a creative writing class.

If these stocks are rising despite a falling Nasdaq or some bad news caused an out of the ordinary dip – i.e. they are not meeting the *tradebits* set forth in the last chapter – I branch out to other selections, not infrequently to health care. Last year, I also day traded with Cigna, Teva, Merck, and Cisco.

So probably my stock picking is actually closer to the eenie meenie minie moe end of the universe than to scholarly due-diligence – but it works.

Chapter 10 - Bears, bulls – and elephants?

"Stop swinging your trunk or you may wake THE BEAR!"

"Hey wait, you can see me?"

Have I been ignoring the elephant in the room? Every financial magazine advises to stick to investing in index funds rather than funds where a human is actively buying and selling stocks. An index fund just passively holds every stock in a particular index, like all 500 stocks in the S&P 500. Or you can choose the Total Stock Market Index fund which contains every single stock traded in the United States. That's owning about 4000 stocks. When the stock market does well, you do well.

The argument is that a hot manager may seem to be achieving higher profits (or smaller losses in bear markets) than the market as a whole through clever stock picking but that over time, this balances out. In fact, the claim is they actually all do *worse* in the long run than index funds do!

Another oft-heard comment: Don't try to time the market. It conveys a similar cautionary warning about the dangers of gambling and greed and outsmarting the powers that be.

I know three others who have told me they have day traded. Two reported they lost money. I do not know how much but at least enough to say they will never do it again. The third – my cousin Gary – says he does well but we have not discussed details. Have I just been extraordinarily lucky as my friend Paul 'Coffee Shop' Bloom (see Chapter 12, *Small Potatoes*) asks me? Or worse, am I only telling you about the wins while concealing losses, either through psychological self-deception or outright intentional deception?

I do not think the success of this strategy is luck. I think the common investing advice does not apply here because this is not investing. Nor is it timing the market. I do think one can get extraordinarily UNlucky which is why for me, the sweet spot has been to put only 20K on the line, just in case. Statistically, the odds of a great tumble at precisely the right second are very low. I don't think that will happen in my lifetime any more than I will win a million-dollar, or even a hundred-thousand-dollar, jackpot in the lottery. Possible, just not likely.

I choose to day trade anyway in the same way I choose to leave the house despite risk of lightning strikes, car accidents, and flying flowerpots.

For smaller losses, let me describe the three worst events and turn the question back to you. Do you consider these to be losses?

One of my three worst trades occurred quite recently while I was writing this book. I was too eager for new data that I could dissect for you. I wanted to introspect more than usual in order to report every single step in the trading process. In fact, because I knew it didn't feel quite right, I bought only five thousand dollars' worth whereas usually for my first trade, I invest double that amount.

It was too early in the day, the NASDAQ had only fallen a little, and the stock was over $38. I had just decided anything under $38 was a bargain so this was not. The inference was based on how the stock had been fluctuating over the past week, from a little under $38 to flirting all the way with $39. I do

not always set such price criteria but if you trade a stock frequently in a short period of time, you will find you get a sense of what is cheap and what is not which can be used to supplement your rules. This fine-tuning is helpful but not necessary.

So in April. I bought 132 shares of TDC at $38.05 for a total cost of $5022.60. I calculated a half percent rise to be 19 cents and set a limit order for $38.24. Later that day it reached exactly $38.24. So it sold? Nope. I have had this happen before, the first time experiencing an almost out of body experience on the phone getting angry with a broker about why a perfectly good order didn't execute. (I'm yelling at a broker? I have a broker? Is this really happening?)

As the saintly broker patiently explained, if everyone wants to sell, there are not enough buyers to go around. There's a line for who goes first that I do not fully understand, another queue I will probably never be at the front of. In any event, it did not sell.

And then it dropped.

Hey Coyote Senior, you were supposed to make your appearance in Chapter 2 when the market fell - stepping off a cliff - remember?

I thought I smelled rabbit nearby, so I came here instead.

By the end of the day, it dropped 2%. The next day, it dropped another 2%!

So I ask you now a question within a question, the word for word identical question I asked in an early chapter "What would you do?" And, "Better question: What would I do? What DID I do?"

First, I edited the limit price to sell at a lower price for a gain of 0.05 percent – basically break even – from the original 0.5 percent. I would not be surprised if every other trader did the same. Next, I bought another $10,000 of the stock, which was now down, after all, nearly five percent. I am guessing maybe half of all traders did this? On the limit price for this trade, I was a coward and only set it to be my usual droll half a percent rise.

Had I set my sights high to a one percent gain, I thought, I could then change the limit order on the fallen stock to half a percent *loss*, which would sell faster, and use the bonus half a percent gain on this new purchase to cancel that loss. But I didn't. A competing thought won out:

"This sure would be stressful if I lost again right now." Something about throwing good money after bad. What exactly does that mean?

The stock quickly rose half a percent and I got my typical profit on that trade. As it turned out, it also exceeded one percent quickly, so the bolder plan would have paid off as well. But it did not reach as high as the new limit price I had set to break even for the original loser.

After this, the price didn't drop - it *tanked*. I tried to buy more of the stock again at the end of the day but missed the 4:30 PM cutoff.

So I did nothing.

Sixteen days later, an email message announced my shares had sold at my break-even limit price. In fact, they would also have sold at the original limit price I had set.

So back to the question I asked at the start of the section. Would you consider this a loss? Technically, no money was lost. But it was choppy and illustrates the hazards of swimming even in the shallow end.

The lesson I learned was that if trading does not feel right but you are really itchy to do so for whatever reason, do not just lower the amount you invest. Also lower that golden half-a-percent goal to a more silver-colored quarter of a percent or even copper tenth-of-a-percent goal.

Of course, if all trades only yielded enough for a tube of toothpaste, it's hard to get excited about stock trading. But in iffy situations, it will still scratch the itch yet not scar the skin.

Chapter 11 - A chapter 11 bankruptcy

Elephants take up space so it is only fitting this one gets an extra chapter. He remains skeptical, "Wait a minute, can't I lose money just as readily as gain it?"

Another occurrence of the three worst trades occurred prior to the tanking Teradata, in 2022. The blunder was apparent immediately. I didn't just bend one of my rules, I positively pulverized it. I took my guideline to trade stocks between $20 and $40 a share and fed it to the sharks.

I bought nearly $5,000 worth of Invitae stock at only $2.66 a share. That's a lot of shares – 1,879 – and a lot of risk. Such cheap stocks are known for their super volatility and risk. I did not buy a penny stock because I was in the mood for a wild joyride, longing to hang on to the surfboard with white knuckles for the half percent ascent – one hopes – in seconds rather than minutes. Nope, as I revealed earlier, I'm boring. Instead, what I held was a grudge, not a surfboard. I was determined to find some way to make up for the greed that is Invitae Corp.

The long story begins with the opposite of Invitae, a wonderful little company that was called Diploid Inc. Did you catch the word 'was'? They were bought out by the evil Invitae. I do not mean I loved to trade Diploid shares. I don't think they even had shares. But their product, Moon, was newsworthy.

Moon analyzed a patient's genome in seconds for every possible rare genetic mutation that might explain mystery symptoms. This included both known

Just because nuts seem
to pop up everywhere

mutations and undocumented ones the software identified as meaningful. Their analysis was based on its altered proteins and nearness to known relevant mutations. The results were ready in seconds, mind you, if you overlooked *that* on first mention. Mere seconds could provide answers to years of suffering!

This little unassuming company, which did not even boast its artificial intelligence (AI) trailblazing, was also generous. They offered affordable pricing for patients. In addition, just my interest earned me some free access, which I used both for research and to help those with limited resources who crossed my path. One such person was diagnosed by Moon as having a type of Ehlers-Danlos Syndrome. I had just started a project with an off-label use of the AI platform.

I was trying to analyze rare mutations in long-lived nonagenarians when the news was broadcast: All accounts would be shut down in 30 days.

But the Invitae buyout was not just shutting down free access; it turns out they were shutting down the whole enterprise. Why? Because they had a competing product. They bought Diploid only to suppress competition, not to integrate a great invention.

It gets worse. Their own product did not offer an analysis of the whole genome. It is also unclear if it provided new mutation discovery. Instead the product provided information on only one gene or small set of candidate genes. Herein lies both the greed and inferiority of Invitae. If clinicians or the patients themselves did not already suspect a candidate gene, the product could not return anything useful. And the evilness: Each focal genetic search was charged separately meaning a desperate patient could be on a fishing expedition that could cost $100,000!

The company's greed in spending too much of their money on bullying buyouts played a role in causing their stock price to tumble from a high of over $50 a share to the couple of George Washingtons I paid when foolishly deciding to try to profit 'from them' out of resentment.

The first foolishness traded as intended, with rapid profit. The second did not. Yes I did this twice...The second time, the volatility brought it down instead, fast, its ensuing waves pushing my target well out of reach. It sank 12% in two days to be specific. And there it stayed. For a harrowing 41 days and 33 minutes. Since the stock did finally reach my sell price, I did not lose any money. But here it was only because I got lucky; I easily could have lost the entire $5,000.

Indeed, a year and a half later Invitae declined to two cents (!) a share and has filed for Chapter 11 bankruptcy. Current stockholders are unlikely to ever see their invested money again.

I don't know what the moral is of this near-death experience. Perhaps it would turn most off of day trading. For me, it was a reminder to not break good tradebits (I also bought it the second the market opened) or do stupid stuff. I will risk a bad saying because it is sort of in keeping with the watery metaphors: Don't throw the baby out with the bathwater.

The third Bad Trade was the first. It occurred during the very first year I ever traded. I think it was a wonderful test of the newly devised strategy. You be the judge.

Before I ever dipped my toe in the water, I went over and over in my mind different aspects of the strategy. I even wondered if it was legal to profit in such a way but could find no info to suggest otherwise. If a stock were to go down instead of up, I reasoned, then the way I would not lose money would be to simply hold the stock rather than sell – for years if I had to. That's why I picked big reputable blue chips that were in many investors buy and hold forever portfolios.

It was AT&T that was to test my resolve. Down it went. Remember back then my goal was a huge one and a half percent gain which made falls more likely. And did my resolve hold?

Yes. I held the stock for....

...eight months. It helps when your

personality includes will power as well as dullness. There were dividends during that time. Messy. But it was not a loss. As far as I was concerned, my strategy survived its test and also helped refine how and what to trade.

And there you have all the losses to do with what you think best. For a baby elephant, see the *post-mortem* at the end but the enormous elephant has left the building.

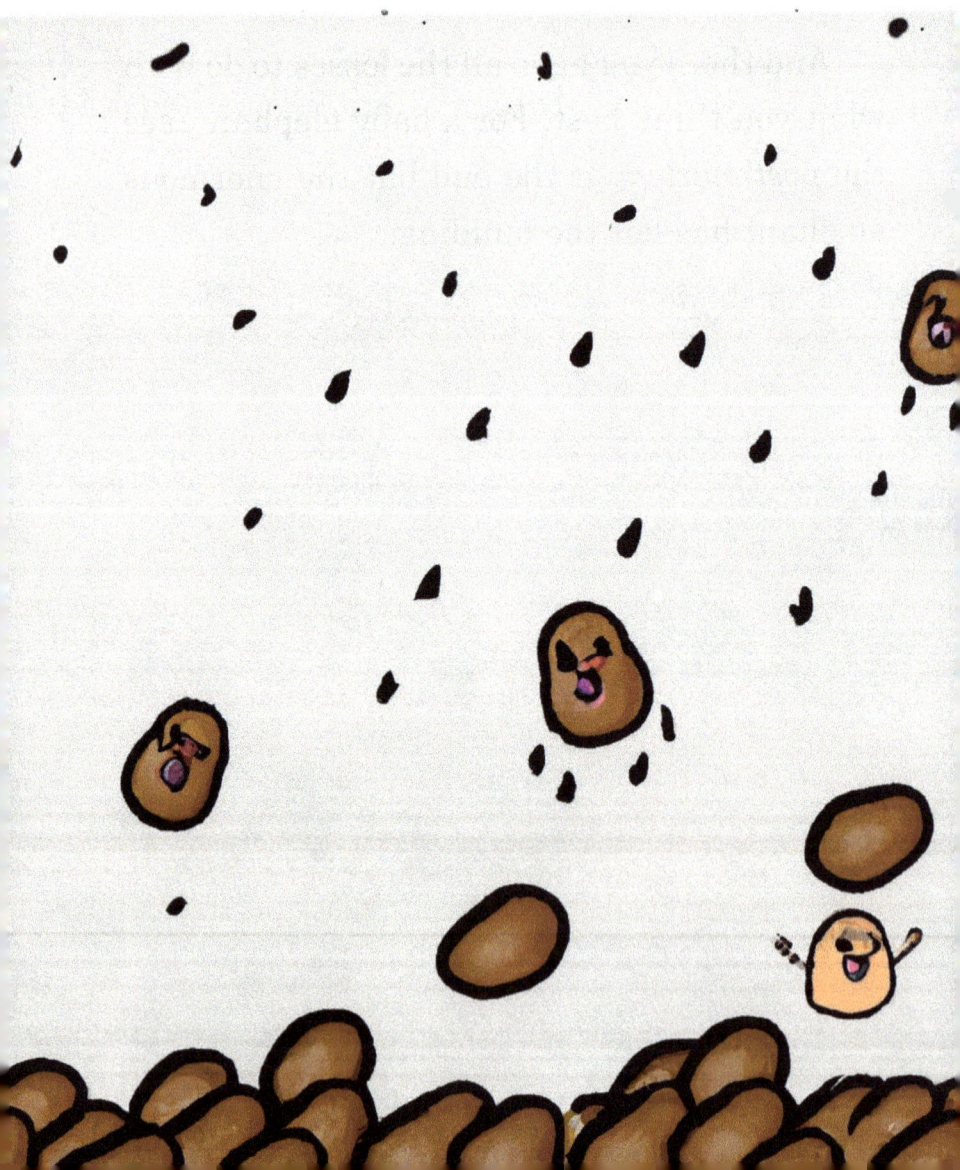

Chapter 12 - Small potatoes

My friend Professor Paul Bloom, the one who put the elephant in the room, has a shortstack called *Small Potatoes*. Don't worry, I don't know what a shortstack is either, unless we are having pancakes. It appears to be new lingua for newsletter, the way trailer parks have become tiny-house communities.

'Small Potatoes' is relevant because that is what we are doing. This is not a get rich quick scheme. This is not a get rich scheme at all.

Last year, I extracted $3,600. With it, I bought a pendulum wall clock, autographed Running Man name tag of my celebrity crush Kim Jong-Kook, symbolic adoption of my favorite wolf, Everblocks (giant Lego-like parts for real building), Netflix, Kardia mobile monitoring, extra grocery deliveries, online cooking class, book on small houses of the 1940s, Polar fitness tracker, extra sandwich deliveries, Turkish towels, express shipping upgrades, three vintage porcelain collies, a magnesium test, handmade felt dog, a stopwatch, test from ZRT lab, extra months of streaming channel Kocowa, a season fruit share, vintage books for a friend whose dad was the illustrator, the cost of an unreturned pair of shorts, Jane Goodall Lego set, blackout curtains, lottery tickets, a contest entry fee, credits for artificial intelligence, leather pouch, and a half dozen more.

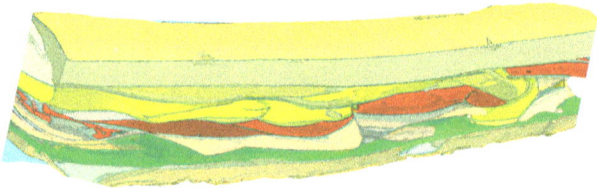

You get the idea.

Would I have bought these things otherwise? No. And even if I did, I would have agonized over whether I really needed each one and if I was getting the best possible type and price. I'm a lifelong saver, not spender. I have never had an interest in much stuff, at least not to keep around for long. (One of my favorite little books is the *Life Changing Magic of Tidying Up* by Marie Kondo who turned obsession into expertise. She discards everything that does not spark joy.)

But these were FREE. I had twin rushes. I indulged my every little whim and they were free. Like in Jeopardy, I gave you the answer first to the question: Why bother?

Everyone likes free stuff. We psychologists (though different specialty) have coined the phrase 'The Power of Free' to capture the finding that subjects in experiments choose worthless free items they do not want rather than pay a very small amount for valuable merchandise. Even luxury brands and upscale restaurants offer two-for-one specials or other promotions knowing full well their customers hardly need the financial handout.

"Turn up your hearing aid again, Sam. It's not shortstack it's, SUBstack, which I like better, but can I please have one of those bill pickles from Chapter 4 to go with my sub?"

But why can't you use this strategy to get rich? Why not multiply everything I have done by a hundred fold? That would at least earn $40,000 a year not $4.000.

For one thing,,40K a year will not make you rich anyway and for another, is setting aside and theoretically risking, however small the risk, $200,000 in your Goldilocks comfort zone? Instinctively, it is not in mine but I have not ruled it out entirely; perhaps when I need big-ticket items I will revisit this.

In any event, free feels really good. And satisfying. The emotions undoubtedly originate from deep evolutionary processes. There are survival advantages to getting gains without expenditure, even if you're winning trinkets not tuition, rubbish, not rabbits.

Chapter 13 - Silver lining

While you won't get rich, there is a cool consolation prize that keeps boredom at bay, provides the hope of a lottery ticket, and the thrill of betting on the horses – all rolled into one.

Once upon a time, there was a little stock that arrived in his new home. But he did not want to grow. Twenty minutes later, an hour later, two hours, four hours; he had not plumped up even a little half a percent. And so he spent a quiet night with his nervous foster parents. The next morning brought sunshine and a surprise. While the guardians were in the shower, he fattened up to nearly TRIPLE what anyone had ever expected. Having overstayed his welcome by just a little, he silently slipped out without troubling anyone just as soon as he could go to market, off for new adventures, leaving in his wake a departing gift for his caretakers to discover.

The day-trading strategy is designed for a very quick sale. But even when it does not do so, and even though the strategy will not get you rich, the silver lining is its potential to bring you an unexpected prize in the mail. Whether because of after-market trading or those lightning-fast first of the morning trades, every now and then you will wake up to a welcome email. Your stock has already sold – and for a price per share *higher* than the half-percent limit order you placed.

The silver lining glimmered on the water this year on a cold late-winter day. At 10:18 AM on March 5, I purchased 278 shares of

TDC at $37.59 for a total of $10,450.02   I put in a limit order of $37.77 aiming for a near half a percent gain.

By the end of the day, it did not sell. I was both surprised and disappointed. It was such a cheap price. The next day, om Wednesday morning, I checked my email:

Dear FOREST BAE,
The following order executed on 03/06/2024 at 9:30 AM, Eastern time:
Account: xxxxxx
Transaction type: Sell
Order type: Limit
Security: TERADATA CORP DEL (TDC)
Quantity: 278 share(s)
Price: $38.28*

I just netted $192 instead of the expected $50! I find a welcome surprise happens on average about once every 20 trades.

The thought of visits by the stock fairy whilst you sleep is more than enough to offset any disappointment or weighty feeling when your day-trading stocks are still around for a sleepover.

Seem Younger!

Jump for Joy!

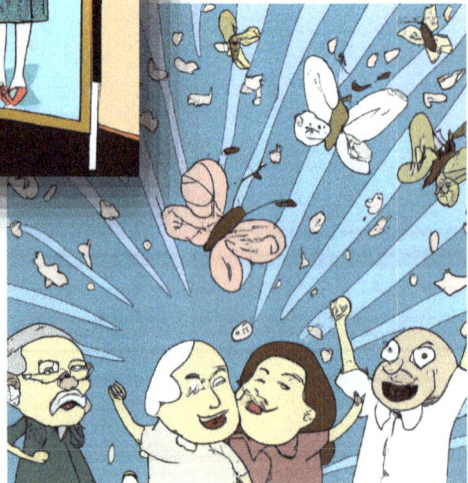

Chapter 14 - Worcestershire sauce

In the 24th episode of Season 4 of the Dick Van Dyke show, 'his' wife Laura gives a recipe for dip to her best friend and next-door neighbor, Millie. Chaos ensues when Laura secretly overhears Millie through an intercom between the homes set up by their kids. Millie is saying to her husband that the dip does not taste right and they suspect Laura intentionally did not tell them one of the ingredients. Laura is outraged and the two couples stop speaking to each other.

By the end of the episode, Laura confesses that she did indeed withhold the special ingredient – Worcestershire sauce – and somehow they all become friends again.

Did I withhold the Worcestershire? Certainly not intentionally. But have a look again at *Goldilocks and the three bears and bulls*. When I bring up the corollary, it starts to get pretty subtle, right? I introduce additional, rather nuanced, considerations about when a *dip* has dipped enough to motivate taking the plunge.

During my latest trades, I have been introspecting for the purposes of this book. That has led to discovering there's quite a few tiny little corollaries that tweak the basic trading rules and which I consider without thinking about it. Perhaps little waves of stock-selling strategies.

Here is a concrete example: You know one of my Goldilocks moments is to avoid trading on Fridays. I don't trade on Fridays – until, that is, I do. I have over the years, on rare occasion, bought a stock late Friday afternoon.

I recently happened to notice on Friday at 3::46 pm that the Nasdaq was down two percent. Very quick check of my usual trading partners found one to have held its own despite the drop but the other had fallen in lockstep with the market. Another quick check, of news this time, did not uncover any special reason for the downturns that would drive me away. That, and knowing the NASDAQ was also generally down for the week, lead me to the conclusion that this was a not to be missed opportunity.

Irrational? Not when considering the reasons behind the rules. No Trade Friday is to avoid hitting a reset button. Come Monday morning, those little waves you're immersed in will get washed away by a new current that is hard to predict. But in this perfect storm situation, it is arguably sensible to now seek out the reset. Ride the tidal wave and capture – by design not happenstance – that sweet *silver liming* (Chapter 13) effect when the market opens at a price well above the half percent limit order placed.

Can the reset go in the other direction? Start Monday sharply lower? Yes, as noted in an earlier chapter. But, if nothing else, I got a stock at a bargain-basement price which shouldn't take too long to at least rise to the original limit price.

So with head in the clouds looking for silver linings, the rest of me has to really scramble before the market closes at 4 pm! There isn't much time. As I enter username and password, I get a message saying too many log-in attempts, reset your password now. Turns out I had misentered my user ID. I am flustered but try to recover and restart my log in. Meanwhile I also started phoning. They are both painfully, really painfully, slow. Internet gets closer first and I hang up the phone.

Click click click click, popup, preview, yes I know, let's go! It's 4:59 and I hit submit! Yes!

A pop-up: 'Warning. The market is now closed. Any trade you place will be implemented when the market reopens.' Nooo!

There's an unexpected downturn, in my mood though, not price. Missed by a matter of seconds.

Science becomes art when there are too

many variables to juggle – or even be consciously aware of. Still though, I believe adhering to all the main tradebits I've set forth is sufficient to syphon coins from the stock market whirlpool. Apprenticeship on my old sofa is welcome but not required. I bet (a half a percent?) you will seem younger, jump for joy, and treat the grandkids now as you are...

...Day Trading for Presents...

And they flew away happily ever after.

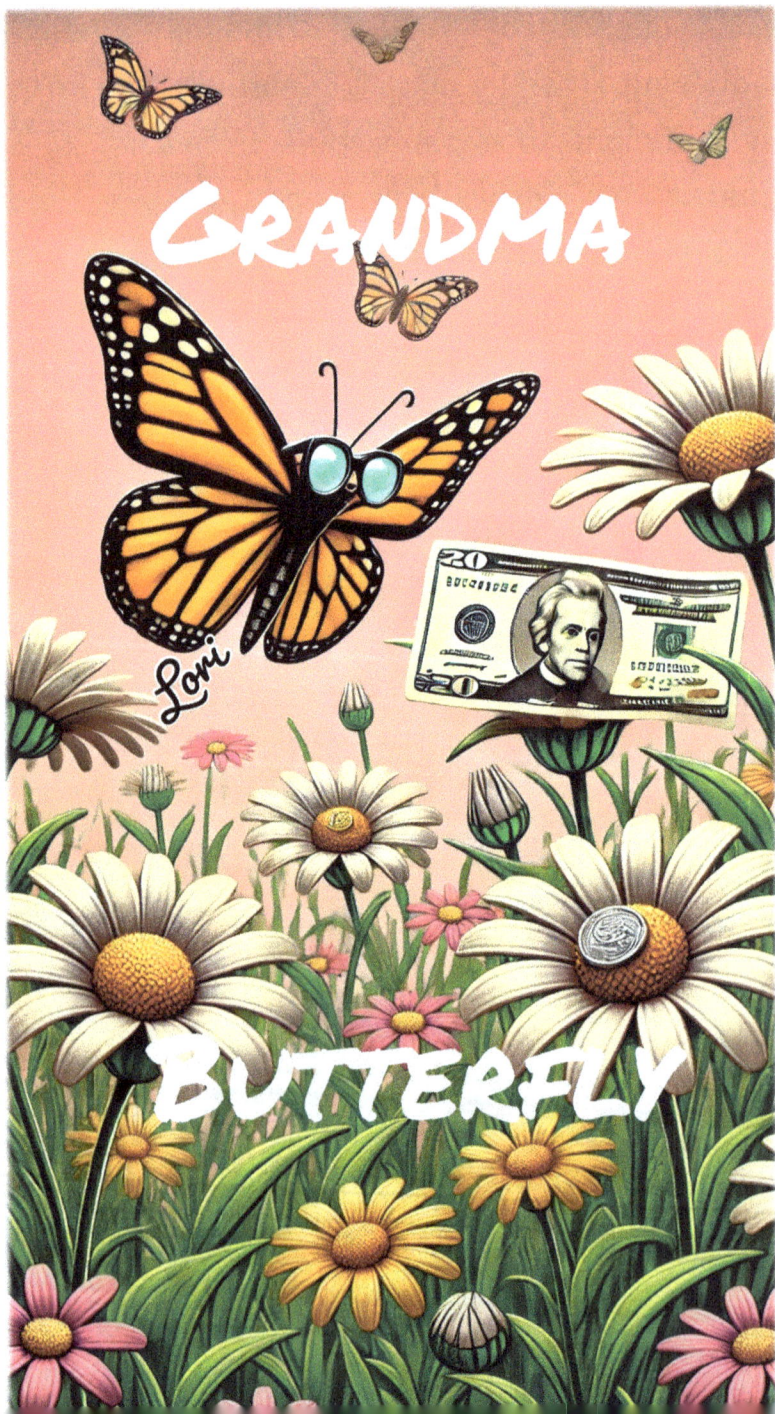

GRANDMA

BUTTERFLY

Post-mortem

I have broken up with Teradata. Ending a long-term relationship is sad. I have since been flirting with Merck, Cigna, Cisco, and Teva until I find another partner. But it had to be done. Teradata was trading at its 52-week low for too long, a bottom that kept getting lower. An investment made five years and kept all this time would have LOST money. Yet I profited through repeated trades. I hear they are switching to a subscription based model and perhaps that will turn things around. I wish you well, Teradata.

The baby elephant referred to in Chapter 11, *A Chapter 11 Bankruptcy*, involves a little math. That is why I saved it for the appendix. The only lectures I ever gave that were universally hated by all my students were on Mathematics in Psychology. They were not shy about conveying their displeasure through exaggerated sighs and heads on desks, like in *Chapter 7's* illustrations. I don't think they appreciated my analysis of the inverse, which I thought clever and exciting: The Psychology of Mathematics! I will try to refrain here and stick just to numbers without opining on what the numbers really mean and feel.

The baby elephant points out that the stock market has done very well recently. In 2023, the S&P 500 gained 26 percent. Wouldn't you do just as well by buying and holding an index fund of the whole thing rather than wasting all that effort repeatedly buying and selling a few stocks? In fact, by popping in and out making yourself dizzy, aren't you doing worse by missing the impressive gains the market made? No and no. Here's why.

For every 10 round trip trades, you are out of the market for 30 days (1 day to trade on average + 2 days for money to clear x 10 trades = 30 days).

During those 30 days, you have earned 5 percent (each 0.5 % profit x 10). So the day-trading rate of return is 60% a year, considerably beating even an outstanding year.

In 2023, had you stayed entirely out of the buy and hold market to day trade instead, you return would be 60% vs. the market's 26%. Had you day-traded just one month (the 10 trades) and been in the buy and hold market for the remaining 11, you would still come out ahead of the market with a gain nearly 29%. (26 - 2.167) + 5 = 28.883). The more you day traded, the higher the return compared to even the stellar market. It's also safer.

And in a downturn? In contrast to 2023, in 2022, the S & P lost 19.4 percent. My return was just as successful in 2022, earning a half a percent a trade in the same amount of time as 2023. A person who day traded just one month whilst keeping the money in the S&P the other eleven would have lost 12.41% (19-(19/12) + 5 = -12.4117) compared to the buy and hold market's loss of 19% and a person who stayed out of the S&P index fund the entire year using the money to day trade instead would be up 60 percent!

I ran out of long weekends before I reached the happily ever after. So if you want an analysis of the size of the little waves in day-to-day stock currents, *drop me a line.* I don't charge commission.

Ah, this just in. There will thankfully be no *post-mortem* for the jackrabbit. It appears Garry the rabbit, AKA Gare Hare, has escaped both the fox *and* the wolf to trade another day.

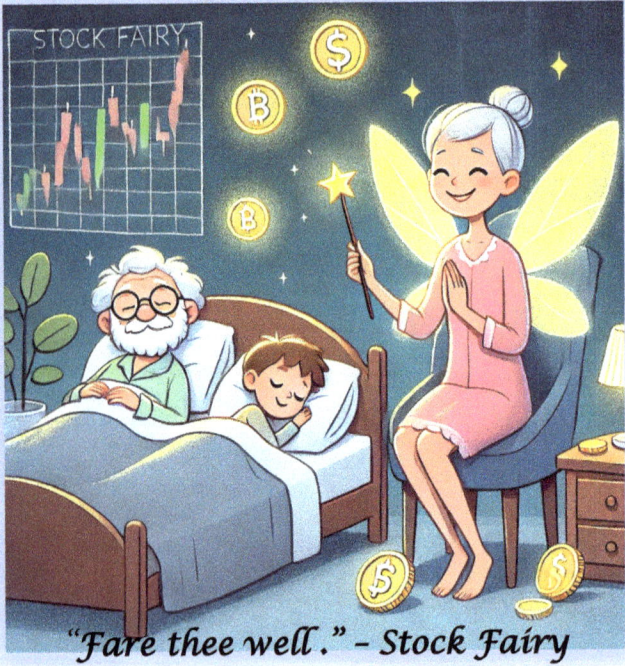

"Fare thee well." – Stock Fairy

www.ingramcontent.com/pod-product-compliance
Lightning Source LLC
Chambersburg PA
CBHW071946100426
42736CB00042B/2295